201

Dear Kenneth,

Caviar is just one of
the many delicious delights
in life, you introduced to me.
I didn't start living
till I met you.

Eternally,
Arlene

The World of Caviar

This edition published in North America in 1999
by CHARTWELL BOOKS, INC.
a Division of BOOK SALES, Inc.
114 Northfield Avenue
Edison, NJ 08837
© Copyright Paris 1999

Translation: Lisa Davidson

ISBN: 0-7858-1084-6
Printed in Spain

The World of

Caviar

Frédéric Ramade

CHARTWELL
BOOKS, INC

Contents

The origins of caviar

Caviar
Antiquity

Sturgeon have flourished in the estuaries and rivers of the Hellenic region since ancient times; the existence of certain archaic tools, such as fish hooks, offer historical proof of this. Furthermore, we know that early on, the Phoenicians and Egyptians discovered the advantages of using salt to preserve fish, which was often the staple food item on board long voyages at sea. References to sturgeon fishing exist in ancient texts by Herodotus, who discussed the plentiful fish in the Dnieper, and in Strabon's writings, which tell us that large quantities of *Acipenser* were caught at Kerch (ancient Panticapaeum). In the fourth century BC, Sopratos of Paphos wrote that the sturgeon taken from the Istros (Danube) were preserved in vinegar, a refined dish that was greatly appreciated by the Scythians. Pliny wrote of the *Acipenser* as a noble fish that was brought to Rome after the second battle against Carthage. It

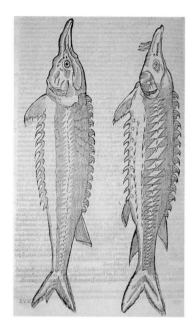

Sturgeon, which has been fished since time immemorial, has always been considered the king of fish.

was served at palatine tables to the sound of trumpets, and the servants wore wreaths in celebration of this "meat of the gods." Athenais also alluded to the noble fish in her writings. Highly prized by the Greeks and Romans, preserved sturgeon would gradually become the sole prerogative of the Byzantines with the decline of the Western empires.

Caviar first appeared in writing in the texts of Diphilus of Siphnos in the third century BC, who spoke of the difference between fresh caviar and salted caviar. References by other authors, including Euthydemus of Athens or Archestratus, lead scholars to believe that caviar, like the meat of the sturgeon itself, was already extremely popular in this distant era. The taste for caviar was so great in the Greek empire that it was imported from the Black Sea and sent to Alexandria, when the city was populated by Greek citizens.

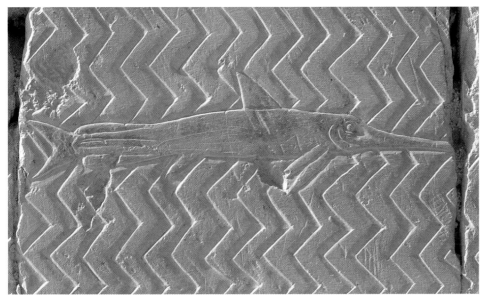

The Romans were great lovers of fish and discovered caviar during their campaigns in Carthage. Four-Seasons Mosaic. Santa Cruz Museum, Toledo.

The Egyptians were the first to use salt to preserve fish. Sturgeon was eaten by the Egyptians, as this bas-relief from the temple of Queen Hatchepsut of Luxor reveals.

Caviar in the Middle Ages and Renaissance

Study of a sturgeon by the Italian painter Pisanello. Red chalk on tinted paper. Louvre Museum, Paris.

Caviar fell into oblivion for several centuries, except in Byzantium, where it was honored and considered a luxury item. This fact is supported by eleventh-century trading registers and by the twelfth-century Greek poems about a refined dish called *caviar*, or *kabiari*, found in Constantinople on the shores of the Black Sea. It gradually returned to Western tables and to treatises starting in the fourteenth century, probably due to Genoese and Venetian merchants, who controlled most of the sea-going trade when caviar first appeared in Italy. The first trace of the word *caviari* appeared in a Latin text dated 1319. The origin of the word is uncertain, but probably comes from the Turkish word *haviar*. The Greeks, however, offer another explanation: they claim it comes from the ancient Greek work *avyarion*, from the root word *avyon*, meaning "egg." In France, the word appeared for the first time in 1432 as *cavyaire*, in a text by Broquière.

At that time, sturgeon were caught in rivers as they swam up-stream to spawn, but this was a fairly unusual event.

Sturgeon fishing was also a strictly regulated occupation. According to a custom that dated to 1370, after the first surgeon of the year was paraded through the streets of Arles, it had to be delivered to the archbishop's dwelling and shared by the local lord, the Porcelet family and the archbishop. Nothing in this report, however, gives any indication about what was done with the roe when a mature female was captured.

Fishing was regulated by a feudal law which stipulated that fishermen operating near the lands of a lord had to pay a fee. The custom was even stricter in England during this same period, where every sturgeon caught belonged to the king.

Certain fourteenth-century texts discuss a game, called the "sturgeon game," played during the Festival of the Tarasque in southern France. A boat was placed on a trailer and filled with water; it was then hauled through the streets by eight horses, while sailors sprayed the crowd with

cavyaire   avyarion

caviari

water to evoke the sturgeon's strong resistance during its capture.

One century later, references to sturgeon and especially to caviar became more specific. Rabelais placed *caviat* from the establishment of Mesire Gaster, the "leading master of the art in the world," on Pantagruel's menu in Book IV. He had probably tasted the precious roe during a trip to Italy several years earlier, where the trade in caviar—as well as capers, chestnuts and cheese—was reserved to apothecaries. Rabelais' laconic allusion to the precious eggs of the sturgeon was fleshed out with details in Cervantes' *Don Quixote*, in which the author vaunted the pleasures of the pressed caviar produced by a traveling monk.

In 1560, Jean-Baptiste Brayerin from Lyon wrote that he enjoyed the salted sturgeon eggs that arrived from Constantinople via Italy, while for the coronation of Pope Pius V in 1566, Scappi, his steward, mentioned a preparation made from "tuna and caviar." By contemporary standards, the methods of preparing and serving

the caviar and sturgeon appear strange to us today—it seems that it was served hot with pepper and bitter orange juice, or cold and spicy. Pope Leo X used to eat trout from Lake Garda accompanied with caviar on slices of grilled bread.

Other anecdotal evidence attests to the scarcity of caviar, such as the story about Galileo, who loved caviar and supposedly sent some to his daughter, a cloistered nun, as a display of his great affection. Unfortunately, the other nuns, unaware of the nature of this precious gift, threw it away, thinking it was cheese from the Netherlands. The passion for caviar was not limited to Constantinople or the other developing towns in Western Europe; ancient records mention that Batu Khan, Ghengis Khan's grandson, enjoyed caviar on candied apples during a visit to the Monastery of the Resurrection at Uglitch, on the banks of the Volga River. According to legend, Turandot's fiancé ate caviar to acquire the strength required to seduce the Chinese princess.

KAVIA

haviar

Sturgeon
tales

A report
dated 14 April 1439

On April 14, 1439, a cortege climbed from the port of Arles toward the Cité (the upper part of the city around the arena) via the narrow pebble-paved street of Cran; flute-players and drummers led this cortege, followed by fishermen carrying a monstrous fish on a plank. The beast was as long as a man, had a greenish-gray back, a pinkish-white belly; the enormous round mouth stretched under his head like that of a shark.

Finally, a triple row of sharp bony plates, like the teeth of a saw, ran along its sides and back. It is what we used to call a *lachen* or *feirou*, today the *esturioun*, the first male sturgeon caught in the territory of Arles this year. Léonard Bruni captured it between the morade of Balquette and the mouth of the Rhône; and Bitronne, the fisherman's mother, walked behind the plank in the company of the town's fishmonger, master Pierre Corinthon. A crowd followed.

Pierre Belon
Of the nature and
diversity of fishes, 1555

Sturgeon produce great income in all countries around the world, but even more in the Black Sea; as it leaves the salt water and enters the Sea of Azov, it is caught heading toward the Tana River (the Danube). The fishermen have their salt ready to salt the roe and the meat, which they place in many large vessels and take to market. These salted eggs are called caviari.

Antonin Carême
The Art of cooking
in the 19th century
(about Russians)

With eggs, they prepare the caviar that they love. They send small barrels of it throughout the entire Russian empire, to Germany and even to Italy. But this ragout made of fish eggs, which are first salted then preserved in oil and vinegar, is not at all suited to the refined and delicate French palate.

Pierre Belon
Travel notes,
(about Turks), 1588

They are "a few special preparations: one is a sort of drug made from the eggs of sturgeon, that everyone calls Caviar, which is common in the meals of the Greeks and the Romans, and everywhere in the Levant; and there is no one who does not eat it, except the Jews, as the sturgeon does not have scales. But those who live along the Tana [Danube], who catch large quantities of carp, separate the eggs and salt them so that they are better than one would usually think, and thereby make red caviar, which is also sold in Constantinople, for the Jews."

Alexandre Dumas
and sturgeons

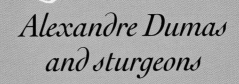

It is possible to appreciate the intelligence of this fish by the manner in which it is caught: the rivers are closed by dams, which is quite easy to do as they are quite shallow. The sturgeon arrive in schools of one thousand to two thousand to swim upstream; as they cannot do so, they swim back and forth in front of the mouth of the river, where huge hooks, hung on cross beams, float two, three or four feet underwater... The fishermen then paddle by boat down the rows formed by the beams across the river, hauling in the sturgeon that have been caught."

Caviar in the
17th and 18th centuries

Russia feu Moscovia itemque Tartaria, *a book dating from 1694, recounts the harvesting of caviar in Muscovia and Tartaria on the Black Sea and the Caspian Sea.*

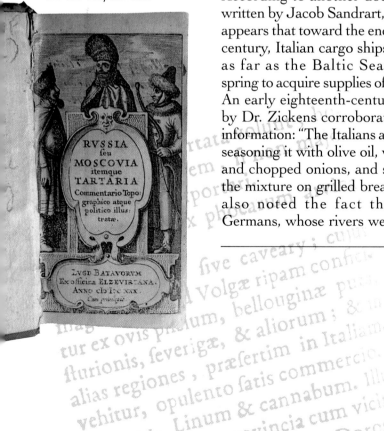

Caviar then fell out of fashion. The Italians alone seem to have retained a taste for caviar over these two centuries, and they continued to spend considerable energy and money to obtain the precious eggs, importing them from Alexandria and Russia. In 1627, Narius reported that the Russians prepared caviar "near the Black Sea, and dispatched quickly to Italy, where they are highly prized." During this period, caviar was preserved in cloth sacks that were buried in the ground along the shores of the Caspian Sea. It remained well preserved due to the high concentration of borax in the soil.

According to another document written by Jacob Sandrart, it even appears that toward the end of the century, Italian cargo ships sailed as far as the Baltic Sea every spring to acquire supplies of caviar. An early eighteenth-century text by Dr. Zickens corroborates this information: "The Italians adore it, seasoning it with olive oil, vinegar and chopped onions, and serving the mixture on grilled bread." He also noted the fact that the Germans, whose rivers were well stocked with sturgeon, had little taste for the delicate flavor of the small black grains that the august doctor described as "greenish-black in color," with a "taste of fish oil." The general distaste for caviar at this time—most often due to ignorance—created an unfortunate diplomatic incident in France: the Russian ambassador ceremoniously offered a spoonful of caviar, a gift from Peter the Great, to Louis XV, who was still a young man, but the nauseous Frenchman spit it out on the carpets of Versailles.

In 1741, Savaray mentioned Kavia in his *Dictionnaire du commerce:* "We are starting to become familiar with it in France, where it is not scorned at the best tables." He also discussed *boutargue*: "... a kind of caviar made from mullet roe; like the other one [caviar], it is highly prized by drunks as a stimulant." This comment reveals the existing prejudices toward caviar in the first half of the eighteenth century, while in the East, intensive fishing in the Black Sea and the Caspian Sea was underway, under the impetus of the Russians.

Buffon's encyclopedia gives the Acipenser *family prominent billing.*

The Czars were great lovers of caviar, while the European Courts turned their noses up at it.

Caviar from
the 19th to the early 20th century

Starting in 1780, the industrialization of the Caspian Sea by John Varvakis, who obtained the fishing rights from Catherine II in return for services rendered, contributed to the reinstatement of the sturgeon, along with caviar, as a gastronomic treat.

Cambacérès, who was Napoleon I's arch-chancellor and Talleyrand's rival, served the emperor an impressive piece of sturgeon placed on "a bed of leaves and flowers." According to a text by Alexandre Dumas: "A concerto of violins and flutes announced its arrival. The flutist, wearing a full chef's outfit, preceded the sturgeon, which was accompanied by four footmen bearing torches, two kitchen assistants with knives at their sides, led by a Swiss guard with halberd in

Preparing caviar on the loading docks, circa 1880.

hand. The sturgeon was placed on a small ladder, eight to ten feet long, which rested on the shoulders of two kitchen assistants. The cortege started to parade around the table to the sounds of the violins and the flute, and amid cries of admiration from the guests."

In 1816, the great chef Antoine Beauvilliers suggested several ways of serving sturgeon, and described a fish that "almost always swims up the great rivers, following the salt ships: several exceptionally fat and long ones have been caught in the Seine." The fish has "neither scales nor bones; its body is armored with a hard skin and covered with bony plates with sharp spikes down the back; there are even two rows of these along the sides." He was also familiar with the Russian passion for caviar: "The Russians make a big fuss over these eggs; the Tartars do a great business; they are extremely expensive in Russia, where the dish is called 'kavia'." Yet Beauvilliers doubted that this "ragout," as he called it, could be recommended to anyone but the "Russians, or to those who have traveled to the

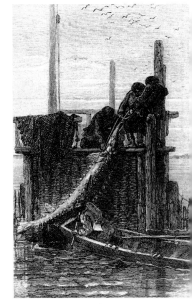

Sturgeon being hauled up onto the pier in the Volga delta, circa 1870.

Sturgeon-fishing on the Caspian Sea. In the middle, one of the ancestors of the Petrossian family, a pioneer in the harvesting and marketing of caviar.

The secret of the finest brands in the late 19th century was to always control production on-site to obtain the best possible quality.

Caviar from
the 19th to the early 20th century

land of the North." He did, however, propose several ways of preparing it in another article in *L'Art du cuisinier*: "Kavia, or sturgeon roe, as the Tartars season it for sale in Russia . . . This is the way to prepare it: take the eggs from one or several sturgeon; the eggs must be perfectly ripe and a small white dot must be visible. Place them in a tub of water. Remove all the fibers, as for veal brains. Using a wooden whisk (used for beating egg whites), beat the roe in the water to remove all the fibers, which will adhere to your whisk. Shake them off and whisk again. When this is done, place the eggs on a flour-sifting sieve, then place the eggs in clean water. Continue beating them and changing the water until all the silt and fibers have been removed. The eggs can then be seen clearly. Let them drain on the sieve and season them with salt and pepper. Mix well and place the roe in a piece of muslin. Tie the four ends of the

cloth and let the eggs drain again. Serve the following day with slices of grilled bread, chopped onions or shallots, and extra salt." It is highly probable that if we were to follow these succinct instructions, we, too, would be disgusted by caviar.

Yet tastes would gradually change and in October of 1856, Léon Godard gave an enthusiastic and well-satisfied account of a meal in a Moscow restaurant called *Trvitza*: ". . . first of all and before the soup, as always, we had caviar accompanied with kummel and *hatchichemé*, a type of flavorful *eau de vie*…"

Alexandre Dumas, in his remarkable *Grand Dictionnaire de cuisine*, offers more practical information concerning caviar, although his text is incorrect in some ways, notably in that he calls caviar the name of a species of sturgeon. Dumas' text describes a trip to the shores of the Caspian Sea, where he spent a month observing sturgeon fishing.

Sampling caviar at the Salon des arts ménagers in Paris in 1928.

Fish merchant's boat in Russia.

A stunning Osetra specimen being hauled up to a fishing hut on the Volga in 1858.

Given the commercial success of sturgeon and caviar, fishing became a bona fide industry. Huge fishing boats gradually replaced smaller craft, a move that jacked up prices.

"This is the most curious kind of fishing; during six weeks to two months, thousands of fish, weighing up to 300 pounds and measuring from 12 to 15 feet in length, are destroyed. In the Danube, sturgeon up to 20 feet long have been caught; they come from the Black Sea and swim upstream to spawn in Baden (in Germany). The flesh of the caviar [sic] has a delicate flavor, rare among cartilaginous fish. It can easily be mistaken for veal. But we must admit that modern nations are not as enthusiastic about this flesh as are older civilizations, who not only wreath this fish in flowers, but bring it to the table to the sound of flutes. With marrow, called visigha, a highly prized pâté is made. But even more highly prized than the marrow pâté are the thousands of eggs collected to make caviar. Kept airtight, the eggs remain fresh. In addition to the eggs that are packed in barrels and shipped the same day [. . .], there are others prepared with salt and shipped later."

The caviar market developed in Italy, but especially in Germany, where the population fell in love with these small salted eggs that had become increasingly difficult to find in local waters, due to overfishing of the sturgeon. The United States began to show interest in caviar starting around 1880, and was able to sell some locally produced caviar, while the rest came from Russian stocks that were sent across the Atlantic.

France caught up in the 1920s, with the efforts of the Petrossian brothers, who imported caviar directly from their home town, Baku, and dealt directly with the new Communist government. Other Russian émigré families tried to develop a local French caviar production in the Gironde region. Since the early years of the twentieth century, caviar has held a place of honor in high society as an exceptional dish reserved for the elite. As a result, a thriving industry has developed. Today threatened by declining stocks of sturgeon due to intensive fishing and the increasing pollution of the main breeding grounds in the Caspian Sea, caviar is more than ever a rare luxury product, and its prices continue to skyrocket.

Caviar:
the sturgeon's
black pearls

A Vast family

The vast sturgeon family has twenty-four species living in fresh and salt waters. • The *Acipenser baeri*, or Siberian sturgeon, with a gray back and white belly, lives in the Lena, Yenisei, Kolyma and Ob rivers, and Zaisan and Baikal lakes. • The *Acipenser brevirostrum*, or Shortnose sturgeon, with a black and olive back and a white underside, inhabits the eastern coast of North America. • The *Acipenser dabryanus*, or small Yangtze sturgeon. • The *Acipenser fulvesceus*, or Lake sturgeon, lives on the eastern shores of the Great Lakes in America and southern Canada. • The *Acipenser gueldenstaedti*, or Russian sturgeon or Osetra, lives in the Danube and Volga rivers, and the Ural and Caspian seas. It can grow as long as 6 feet and 6 inches and weigh as much 440 lbs. • The extremely rare *Acipenser kikuchii*, or Japanese sturgeon, lives in southern Japan. • The *Acipenser medirotris*, or Green Sakhalin sturgeon, is found in the seas off Alaska, California, China,

The front end of the Acipenser gueldenstaedti *or Russian sturgeon, also called Osetra.*

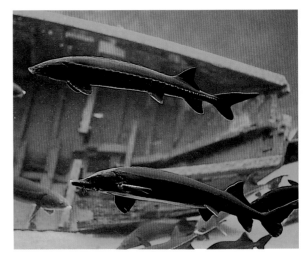

The Acipenser baeri, *or Siberian sturgeon, live in fresh waters.*

The vast sturgeon family counts over twenty-four different species.

Old engraving depicting an Osetra.

The Acipenser shrenki, *or Amur River sturgeon.*

Sturgeons form
the Chondrostei *group
of fishes, which
are regrouped under
the various acipenseroid
families.*

The Acipenser stellatus *(foreground), the* Acipenser gueldenstaedti *(middle) and the*
Huso huso *(background) respectively produce sevruga, osetra and beluga.*

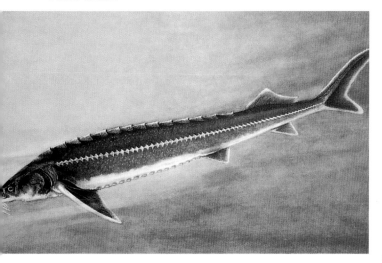

The Scaphyrhynchus platorynchus, *or Shovelnose sturgeon, is found in the*
United States.

The Acipenser brevirostrum, *or Shortnose sturgeon, is present*
in North America.

This sturgeon, with its elongate nose, is an Acipenser stellatus, *or Stellate stur-*
geon, commonly known as Sevruga.

A Vast family

Japan, Korea and Russia. Its flesh is not edible.

- The *Acipenser multiscutatus*, found in southern Japan.
- The *Acipenser naccarii*, or Adriatic sturgeon, with a short, rounded snout, inhabits the Po River in Italy.
- The *Acipenser nudiventris*, or Ship sturgeon, inhabits the Aral and Caspian seas.
- The *Acipenser oxyrinchus*, or Atlantic sturgeon inhabits the United States Atlantic coast.
- The *Acipenser ruthenus*, or Sterlet, with a beige-gray back and sides, lives in the Black Sea, the Sea of Azov and the Caspian Sea.
- The *Acipenser shrenki*, or Amur River sturgeon.
- The *Acipenser sinensis*, or Chinese sturgeon, lives in the Yangtze River system and the Yellow Sea.
- The *Acipenser stellatus*, or the Sevruga or Stellate sturgeon, lives in the Black Sea, the Sea of Azov and the Caspian Sea. It has a star pattern along its black-gray back.
- The *Acipenser sturio*, or Altlantic (Baltic) sturgeon is found off the coast of Portugal and Scandinavia, and in the Riani River basin in the Black Sea.
- The *Acipenser transmontanus*, or White sturgeon, lives in the Columbia River and along the Pacific coast of the United States.
- The *Huso dauricus*, or Kaluga sturgeon, lives in the Amur River.
- The *Huso huso*, or Beluga sturgeon, inhabits the Caspian and Black seas.
- The *Pseudoscaphirynchas kaufmanni*, or Large Amu-Dar shovelnose sturgeon, inhabits the Aral Sea.
- The *Pseudoscaphirynchas hermanni*, or Small Amu-Dar shovelnose sturgeon, inhabits the Aral Sea.
- The *Pseudoscaphirynchas fedtschenkoi*, or Syr-Dar shovelnose sturgeon, lives in the Syr-Dar River.
- The *Scaphyrhynchus albus*, or Pallid sturgeon, lives in the Mississippi River.
- The *Scaphyrhynchus platorhynchus*, or Shovelnose sturgeon, inhabits the Mississippi and Missouri rivers.

Only three species are industrially fished for caviar: the *Huso huso*, or Beluga; the *Acipenser gueldenstaedti*, or Osetra; and the *Acipenser stellatus*, commonly known as Sevruga.

Sturgeon were among the first fish to inhabit the oceans covering the planet 300 million years ago.

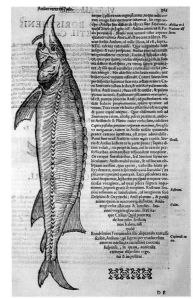

The Acipenser sturio, *or Atlantic (Baltic) sturgeon, was once abundant in France's Garonne, Gironde and Rhône rivers.*

Acipenser stellatus, *or Sevruga, is also called the Stellate sturgeon due to the star pattern along its back.*

Sturgeon-fishing has existed since time immemorial. It dates back to approximately 12,000 BC, according to recently discovered documents.

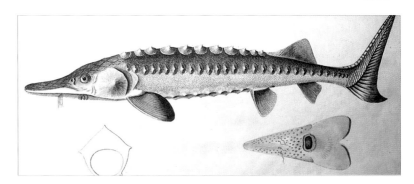

For years, scientists and naturalists sought to classify the various sturgeon species. The German naturalist Ludwig Brehm's splendid Life of the Animals was published in Leipzig in 1884.

The Huso huso, also called Beluga, is the largest of the sturgeon and can weigh up to one ton.

The Growth cycle
of sturgeon

Opposite page:
Spot-checks are required
to make sure that the
fish are not juveniles.

S turgeon have a fairly long life cycle. If they manage to escape the nets and poles of the fishermen, they can reach and even exceed one hundred years of age.

They primarily eat worms and roots at the bottom of rivers and seas, burrowing with their projecting snouts and barbels. The sturgeons of the *Huso* family (*Huso huso* and *Huso dauricaus*) are the only ones that also can eat fish smaller than themselves, as a complement to their feeding habits. The Beluga sturgeon have large short heads and mouths that are so wide they can swallow entire salmon with one gulp. Female sturgeon of the smaller species reach sexual maturity around the age of 5 to 9 years; the larger ones reach maturity from the age of 8 to 14. The males of the same species, however, reach maturity some three to four years after the females.

Abusive fishing methods prevent the young sturgeon from reaching maturity.

The barbels underneath the fish's mouth permit it to detect food.

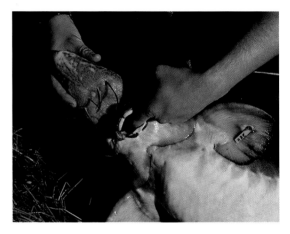

Sturgeon feed primarily on worms and roots.

Females reach sexual maturity between the ages of 5 and 14 years depending on the species. Some can reach the age of 100.

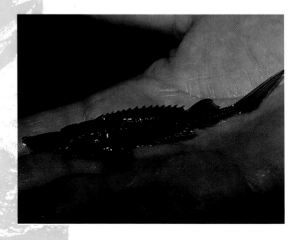

The Reproduction

of sturgeon

Sturgeon reach the required level of sexual maturity for the maturation of the eggs at age 8.

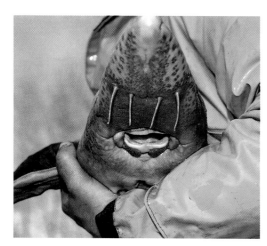

Certain freshwater species are now bred on fish farms.

Most sturgeon species are marine fish that enter fresh water rivers to spawn. Sturgeon that live in fresh water lakes are the result of species that were trapped in inland lakes formed at the end of the ice ages; they then adapted to this new environment. During the reproductive cycle, the female sturgeon, which reaches sexual maturity between 8 and 14 years of age, looks for a place to spawn, generally in a depression in the river, a sea bed or sheltered area in deep water, where she can deposit the eggs that will be fertilized by a male. As she has gained a great deal of weight at this age of sexual maturity and with the eggs, she therefore avoids the river's strongest currents. A number of smaller male sturgeon swim around her as she seeks a suitable place to deposit her eggs.

Once the eggs have been deposited and fertilized, they develop into fry that continue to grow in fresh water before swimming out to the salt-water environment.

Female sturgeon can be fertilized and produce caviar between 8 and 14 years of age.

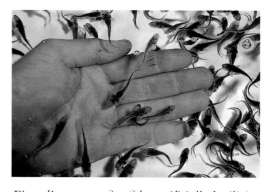

Fingerlings are produced by artificially fertilizing the eggs.

Breeder Jacques Carré, in the Gironde, opted for the Acipenser baeri, *a Siberian sturgeon.*

Using fish-breeding methods, the fingerlings can develop without being exposed to the risks of natural predators and fishing. A great number reach maturity.

Sturgeon inhabiting freshwater lakes are actually the descendants of fish which remained trapped after the retreat of the ice during the glacial periods and adapted to their surroundings.

Fishing zones

The Caspian Sea

The Caspian Sea is the largest inland sea in the world, with a surface area of 438,000 square kilometers. The Aral-Caspian depression is situated between the Caucasus to the west, the Ustyurt plateau to the east and the Elburz range to the south. The sea borders Russia, Iran and the three countries that were part of the former USSR—Azerbaijan, Kazakhstan and Turkmenistan. Before coming under Russian control in the ninth century, the Caspian Sea was occupied by a population that has since disappeared, the Khazrs, who were excellent traders.

The Caspian Sea consists of three basins: the shallow northern basin; the central basin with an average depth of 574 feet; and a southern basin, with an average depth of 1,066 feet, although depths of up to 3,281 feet have been recorded. The water temperature ranges widely, from 30° F in winter (in the north) to nearly 80° F in the south, during the summer months. The salt content is about 12 parts per 1,000 by weight.

The Caspian Sea is the greatest sturgeon reserve in the world.

The Caspian Sea
bordering Iran

A Turkmenian fisherman from the area near Gorgan. The Turkmenians are from the steppes of Central Asia but they have a solid background as sailors.

The southern part of the Caspian Sea is also its deepest area; sturgeon fishing therefore developed in this region relatively late. Furthermore, Iran is a Muslim country, and the dietary laws of the religion (like the Jewish religion) prohibits fish without scales from the diet. Sturgeon fishing and caviar production developed in the Gilân and Mazandarân regions under the influence of nearby Russia, which has always tried to extend its control over the northern provinces of the Persian empire. From 1888 to 1925, the Russian company Lianosov held a concession for fishing in the area; during this period, it paid 10 million rubles for fishing rights. In 1928, after Shah Pahlavi came to power (with the help of dissident Cossack troops), a joint Soviet-Iranian company, known as Mahi-Iran, was created. But the deal still favored the Russians, who reaped the benefits of most of the caviar and fish production.

A well-deserved rest in the SHILAT complex, Iran's state fisheries company. Fishermen spend the entire fishing season in the company housing units, then return to their families for the remainder of the year.

The morning prayers take priority over every other ritual.

The village
of Shahpoqli
on the banks
of the Caspian Sea.

The Turkmenian city
of Gomishan, with its
Russian-style wooden houses.

The nets are hauled up twice a day. In between, the fishermen keep an eye on the nets or repair them.

In the early morning, the long stream of flat-bottomed boats leave the fisheries and head out to the open seas to haul up the nets.

The Caspian Sea
bordering Iran

In 1953, a new Iranian fisheries company was developed, which still grants one-third of the income from its caviar production and most of the sturgeon to Russia. The agreement signed at the time was still linked to the initial Russian investment in the Iranian fishing industry. Muhammad Reza Pahlavi, the despotic young Iranian ruler, was proud of his country's caviar production, and it became one of Iran's prestige products, along with carpets and oil. Luxurious banquets organized in honor of Western guests always include impressive amounts of the best-quality caviar. After the Iranian revolution, Ayatollah Khomeini allowed caviar production to continue and decreed that sturgeon could be eaten. Yet the context was different and a new company, the SHILAT, was created as a state monopoly on fishing in Iran. Every two or three years, it sells its future catch to the highest bidder on the European, American and Asian markets. This dealer then acquires exclusive rights to the sale of Iranian caviar in his specific sector. Today, due to technical progress accomplished by the Iranians and to the dismantling of the former Soviet Union, Iranian caviar is considered to be one of the best, although the production levels remain far below those of the Russians.

*The raising of the nets at dawn.
The crew which brings back females
with eggs receives a bonus.*

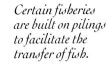

*Certain fisheries
are built on pilings
to facilitate the
transfer of fish.*

*The main fishing
seasons are late
winter and fall.*

The Caspian Sea
bordering Iran

Right: Many rivers flow into the Caspian Sea. Sturgeon love to congregate in the riverbed.

Once unloaded, the fish are then scrubbed. Some specimens, such as beluga, can reach up to 6 meters in length and can weigh up to a ton. Its caviar is the most prized.

The primary fishing zones are situated around the Gorgan Gulf to the east, an area with a large population of Turkmen; and the Anzali Gulf to the west. Many other smaller areas, however, are scattered along the coast. The caviar is processed on site, while the sturgeon are sent to Anzali, where they are frozen and sent to foreign markets. The fisheries are strictly controlled and the fishermen live in collective housing units that seem to be a throwback to the kolkhoz era of the nearby former Soviet Union. For some twenty years now, Iran has worked alongside Russia to increase the sturgeon population. The country has two immense fish hatcheries where the sturgeons are fertilized artificially. The fry are raised in the hatcheries and released into the sea when they are old and large enough to survive.

White caviar, which was once offered as the ultimate luxury to the court of the Shah of Iran, comes from albino fish. Its taste is somewhat bland, and there is somewhat less of a demand for white caviar.

Displaying the wares in an Iranian bazaar circa 1910.

When the fish cannot be treated quickly, they are stored in large boats filled with salt water.

The fish is quickly brought back to the fishery and hoisted up onto a conveyor for preparation.

The Caspian Sea bordering Russia

The primary fishing zone in the Caspian Sea is situated in Russian territory. Historically, it has been centered around the Volga River basin, where nearly 75 percent of the total sturgeon catch of the Caspian comes from. Other less important areas include the Astrakhan and the Baku river basins. Until the Russian revolution, fishing rights in the regions under Russian control were granted by the Czars, in exchange for huge sums of money. With the creation of the Soviet republic, the country's entire caviar production was placed under the control of a single institution, the V/O Prodintorg, which exported the caviar by boat from Leningrad, then by airplane and truck from Moscow, Guryev and Astrakhan to Central and Western Europe. A few problems appeared in the 1960s with the construction of dams on the Volga River, which prevented certain species, including the beluga, from swimming upstream to reach their usual spawning areas.

The catch is quickly processed on specially equipped boats on the Volga delta.

The Caspian Sea bordering Russia

Despite problems due to pollution and construction projects upstream on the river, the Volga remains one of the main fishing zones on the Caspian Sea.

In response to this problem (as well as that of over-fishing, due to increasing demands for caviar), the Russian government has launched an ambitious program to restock sturgeon. Artificially fertilized fry were raised in basins before being freed in their natural seas. Their efforts have been successful—nearly 90 percent of the beluga caught today comes from the fish hatcheries. Yet the sturgeon population is still progressively declining, and with the dismantling of the Eastern bloc countries and the creation of the new countries of Kazakhstan, Azerbaijan and Turkmenistan, the situation has become even more complicated, with increasing pollution and ineffective controls on poaching. The Russian legacy, responsible for the development of high-quality caviar in Russia and neighboring countries, is no longer what it once was, and the risks to the sturgeon population and to caviar production in the Caspian Sea are more worrisome than ever.

The fishing nets pull in other species of fish, but the sturgeon is immediately identified by its size.

The sturgeon are carefully sorted before being sent to the treatment plant.

In Astrakhan, sturgeon are opened up and transported on a conveyor belt to the caviar section of the treatment plant.

Industrialization often upsets the ecology and the culinary joys of life. The unsettling smokestacks of the Gazprom factory located on the banks of the Volga are a menace to the survival of the sturgeon.

Once the precious eggs have been removed, the fish are stocked in refrigerated units, such as this one in Atyrau, Kazakhstan, before being treated and shipped off.

Other sturgeon habitats

Opposite page: Lake Baikal, the largest freshwater body in the world, is inhabited by a large colony of Acipenser baeri, or Siberian sturgeon. This is the species raised by fish-breeders in the Girondin region of France.

In winter, Lake Baikal freezes over. During years of extremely cold temperatures, trucks can travel over the thick layers of ice.

Even if today most important place for sturgeons remains the Caspian sea, there exist less important fishing zones worth mentionning. The Amur river, common to China and Russia, provides four species of sturgeons, including the largest one, favorable to caviar production; it is the Kaluga, or *Huso dauricus*, which can commonly reach up to 20 feet and weigh 2,000 pounds. Fed by 336 rivers, Baikal lake in Siberia is the deepest lake on earth. It is an important fish tank, where *Acipenser baeri*, or siberian sturgeon can be found. As for the Lena river, also in Siberia, even if it is frozen most of the year, sturgeon fishing is possible. Lastly, the Yangsi Jiang, the longest river in China, also has sturgeons, particularly two species, the *Acipenser sinensus*, or chinese sturgeon, and the *Acipenser dabryanus*, or small Yangzi sturgeon.

Two species of small sturgeon inhabit the majestic Yangtze Gorges in China, but unfortunately they are not good for caviar production.

The sturgeon population in Siberian rivers like the Lena is dropping off more and more each year as hydroelectric dams are being built.

The Black
Sea

Opposite page:
A sturgeon fisherman
in Vilcovo (Romania)
prepares his hooks.

Extracting the roe in Vilcovo, Romania, circa 1934.

Sturgeon fishermen
in the winding canals
of the Danube near
Vilcovo, Romania,
circa 1934. The small
town, built primarily
of wood, was
prosperous and
the caviar tins were
meticulously
prepared.

The second-leading caviar-producing region after Russia (primarily by Romania), the Black Sea is no longer a major source of sturgeon. The annual production, which had once been nearly 18 tons, has dropped to less than 4 tons today.

The primary fishing zone was situated in the Danube River delta, particularly around the town of Vilcovo. Many Russian emigrants, including the Lipovans, who had a perfect understanding of how to prepare caviar, fled the repression under Peter the Great. Fishing continues today, despite an urgent need to protect the stock of wild sturgeon and to develop a joint repopulation and hatchery program with the participation of the Moldavians and the French. Romanian caviar is therefore sold cheaply on the local market or is sold as contraband, rarely reaching the Western European markets. The solution resides in retraining the fishermen to work in hatcheries, but the political and economic problems of the country are such that this is not a feasible option.

Filtering the eggs is a crucial step in preparing caviar. It is a simple process, yet requires great dexterity to avoid breaking the fragile pearls.

The United States

Americans acquired a taste for caviar later than elsewhere, even though the coastlines and many lakes are filled with sturgeon. Around 1850, sturgeon roe was used as bait for lobster pots, and it was not unusual to see a piece of bread slathered with caviar and served with a beer in New York bars. American gourmets only started to show an interest in caviar around 1880. Some of the caviar was imported from Germany, and local production began to develop more strongly. In 1897, caviar production on the Delaware River and Delaware Bay was recorded to be 267,000 pounds. This development was short-lived, however; by 1904, the records show that the production in the states of Delaware, New Jersey and Pennsylvania had dropped to just 15,927 pounds.

This decline was probably the result of overfishing due to a lack of regulation and knowledge about sturgeon, as reflected in a Commerce Department decree dated April 1916, entitled "What is caviar and how to prepare it." This paper was intended for fishermen who, if they caught female sturgeon, would then know how to prepare the caviar. It described the tools required, stressing the quantities and qualities of salt, followed by the filtering and packaging stages, marketing and finally, labels to correctly identify the caviar. The sturgeon recommended for caviar production were the Common sturgeon (on the east coast), and the white Oregon sturgeon (*Acipenser transmontanus*).

New programs have recently been set up to battle pollution and to promote larger sturgeon populations; if successful, American caviar production could be expanded significantly, to reach the considerable sum of 25 tons per year.

A fish dealer exhibiting a superb sturgeon caught in Florida's Indian River in 1902.

American caviar production is booming following a steady campaign to boost the sturgeon population.

France

In 1890, a German trader named Schwab traveled to the Gironde region, where sturgeon eggs were available. When Schwab realized that the local residents used the sturgeon roe as bait for eel and sardine fishing, he quickly offered to purchase the eggs.

Yet the industry only took off with the arrival in the region of a White Russian, M. Scott, commissioned by the Prunier firm of Paris. M. Scott, who appointed a production manager for caviar production in each port, drove all through the area monitoring the sturgeon catch. Starting in the 1940s, new Russian emigrants started looking for a share of the market by purchasing Gironde-produced caviar for their brands (La Volga, Kaspia, Sutrakof). The caviar from the *Acipenser sturio* in the Gironde was velvety and had a nutty flavor. In 1922, the records in Podensac (upstream from Bordeaux) note an estimated production of 6.8 tons. This figure was around 5 tons in the 1950s, nearly one-fourth the national consumption; it plummeted to 250 kilos in 1963, then to 25 kilos in 1980. Although there have been highly successful periods, sturgeon fishing has never been widespread in France, given the scarcity of the fish and the cost of the licenses. In the 1950s, sturgeon fishermen represented about one-tenth of the total catch of fish. Yet in 1958, about one hundred fishermen were registered, for total sales representing 2 to 3 million francs at the time—or enough for fishermen to live on for most of the year. For the residents of the Gironde, sturgeon were considered money in the bank. Fishermen worked primarily in the

Jacques Carré is a fish-breeder in the Gironde, a region that produced wild caviar until the late 1960s.

A fine sturgeon caught in the Dordogne in 1925.

Jacques Carré set up his hatchery in former salt marshes.

France

estuary of the Gironde, using lightweight boats with oars and a sail. On board were one or two men, and the ship had 120-meter-long, 3-meter-high nets. Three other types of boats were also used to sail upstream: the lightweight, narrow *filadière*, with a shallow hull and fitted with an awning under which two or three men could be sheltered; the yole or round-hulled skiff; and the flat-bottomed dinghy.

The fishing season began on March 15 and mobilized the efforts of most of the region's fishermen, as described in this document: "In the ports from which the *filadières* sailed in search of the mythical fish — from Talmont, Mortague, Port-Maubert, Callanges, Marmissan — people still talk about the extraordinary era of the *créa* [the local word for sturgeon in southwest France] and caviar, of the "magical fishing nets, the miraculous sturio catches."

In addition to the Garonne and the Gironde rivers, the Rhône was also teeming with sturgeon. Indeed, Arles, Avignon and Montélimar prospered greatly from sturgeon fishing. The last catch in Montélimar, however, dates to 1913. This gradual disappearance in the early twentieth century was caused by overfishing and a modification of the riverbeds to accommodate river traffic (construction of embankments that created faster currents). As early as the turn of the century, specialized articles were already discussing the possibility of restocking the rivers with sturgeon fry. The increasing pollution of the river, with the advent of chemical industries, effectively halted any proposals to return sturgeon to the Rhône River.

Today, the production of French caviar is limited to a few small hatcheries in the Gironde River basin, where Siberian sturgeon are being acclimatized with the intention of relaunching the "Girondin caviar" label.

In the Gironde region, as elsewhere, processing the eggs is an extremely meticulous operation.

Huge sturgeon sometimes swim up the Rhône before the bed is ready, and thus prevent spawning.

Caviar from the Gironde region now has a "Girondin caviar" label, or appellation contrôlée, like Iranian and Russian caviar.

Fishing techniques

Lines
and ropes

This technique, used in the past by the Cossacks and the residents of Astrakhan, has completely disappeared. Fishermen attached pieces of woven horsehair with hooks to a long rope; the hooks were then baited with whitefish. The rope was threaded through stones with holes in them, which held the cord on the bottom of the river or sea bed. One of the ends was also attached to the bottom or tied to a tree on the bank. Wooden floaters were attached by lighter lines, so that fishermen on the surface could detect when a beluga had been hooked.

The fishermen moved their boats over the fish and hauled it up using the rope and a fishhook. The sturgeon was stunned quickly so that it could not tip the boat. Unloaded on the docks, the sturgeon was immediately cleaned and prepared.

Once the fish has been hooked and hauled in, it must quickly be stunned so as not to tip the boat.

Once hoisted up onto the boat, the fish must be brought ashore as quickly as possible so as not to damage the precious eggs.

Extracting the roe and filtering the eggs on the loading dock on the banks of the Volga, early twentieth century.

This engraving from the late nineteenth century perfectly illustrates the line fishing technique. It also reveals the abundance of sturgeon in the great rivers of Central Europe at the time.

Many hooks are attached to a long rope at fixed intervals, then the rope is dropped to the bottom of the water.

Fixed nets and drag-nets

Most sturgeon fishermen these days use nets. Some are "fixed"—in other words, they are placed perpendicularly to the bank and hauled in once or twice a day; most Iranian fishermen use this technique. The other type of net is the "drag-net," which is dragged behind a trawler; this is the most common technique in Russia. Fixed nets are tied to floaters and weighted down with stones. This ancient technique was described by Pierre Belon in a text about sturgeon fishing in the Pau River: "We catch them in the Pau with nets that have gourds tied to them instead of cork; they are then thrown across the river into the water."

Once trapped in the net, the sturgeon are hauled in alive and placed in the well of the boat. They are immediately placed on their backs and taken as quickly as possible to the processing plants. When the fish are too large, they are left in the water; the fishermen string a rope through the mouth and gills and tow the fish behind the boat.

Above: Sturgeon fishing in Astrakhan in 1930.

Opposite page: Boats are equipped with fish-wells for storing the fish. Mouth of the Volga.

Sturgeon fishing on the banks of the Volga. Fishermen are bringing in their nets.

A fisherman in Astrakhan proudly displays his freshly caught sturgeon.

Fixed nets

When sturgeon fishing still existed in France, it was practiced, according to Roule, "using special nets, named *'claro,'* with a mesh of 8 inches; they were 262 feet long and 16 feet deep. The season, later than in the Atlantic rivers, started in April and May and ended in July or August." Jourdain added to this description of fishing in the Gironde and Garonne rivers with the following text: "The weighted net, held in place vertically by floaters, is placed in the water behind the boat, perpendicular to the current of the incoming tide. The two ends are brought together and tied to a wooden rod or 'mambo' held by the fisherman. The boat then drifts with the current. The fisherman can detect when fish are caught in the net through the movement of the mambo. The prey is then hauled on board or lashed to the side."

Through the 1950s, these nets, called trammel nets, were made by hand. The multi-layered net had an inner net, 4 to 8 inches across, and an outer net with a much lar-

A fisherman immersing the net.

The nets have been cleaned and repaired in preparation for the next fishing season.

Each fishing season, the fishermen cast out the net in a traditional ritual.

ger mesh, 2 feet across or more. The nets were woven using large acacia-wood needles. Lead weights were then sewn along the net to weigh down the lower edge, and cork was attached to the upper edge. The dimensioning of the mesh was considered a highly skilled technique and essential to a good catch. It was not unusual for certain fishermen to spy on the work of more successful colleagues.

Above and below: Once the fish's gills are snared in the net, the sturgeon is hauled up onto the boat by the fisherman.

It is sometimes tricky for fishermen to remove the fish from the net.

Ice fishing
and harpoons

It is so cold on the ice floes that the fish do not need to be refrigerated. The Mille Lacs region of Minnesota.

Of all the different fishing techniques, the harpoon is the least advisable if the fisherman intends to make caviar from the precious sturgeon roe. This technique was once used by the Cossacks, who called it *bagornaya*. It is still popular in North America, particularly in the middle of winter on Lake Minnesota, when a thick layer of ice covers the entire lake. The fishermen cut holes in the ice — beginners may make it a simple round hole, while experienced fishermen cut a square hole and place a heated shelter over it. The fisherman waits long hours for the fish to surface, at which point he harpoons it and hauls it up onto the ice. Aside from the damage done to the flesh of the fish, this technique damages the eggs, as the sturgeon releases a toxic substance when it is threatened.

Each of these small huts has a trap-door in the floor through which fishermen harpoon fish.

A Russian fisherman in the early twentieth century.

Sturgeon are no longer harpooned, as this technique damages the precious roe.

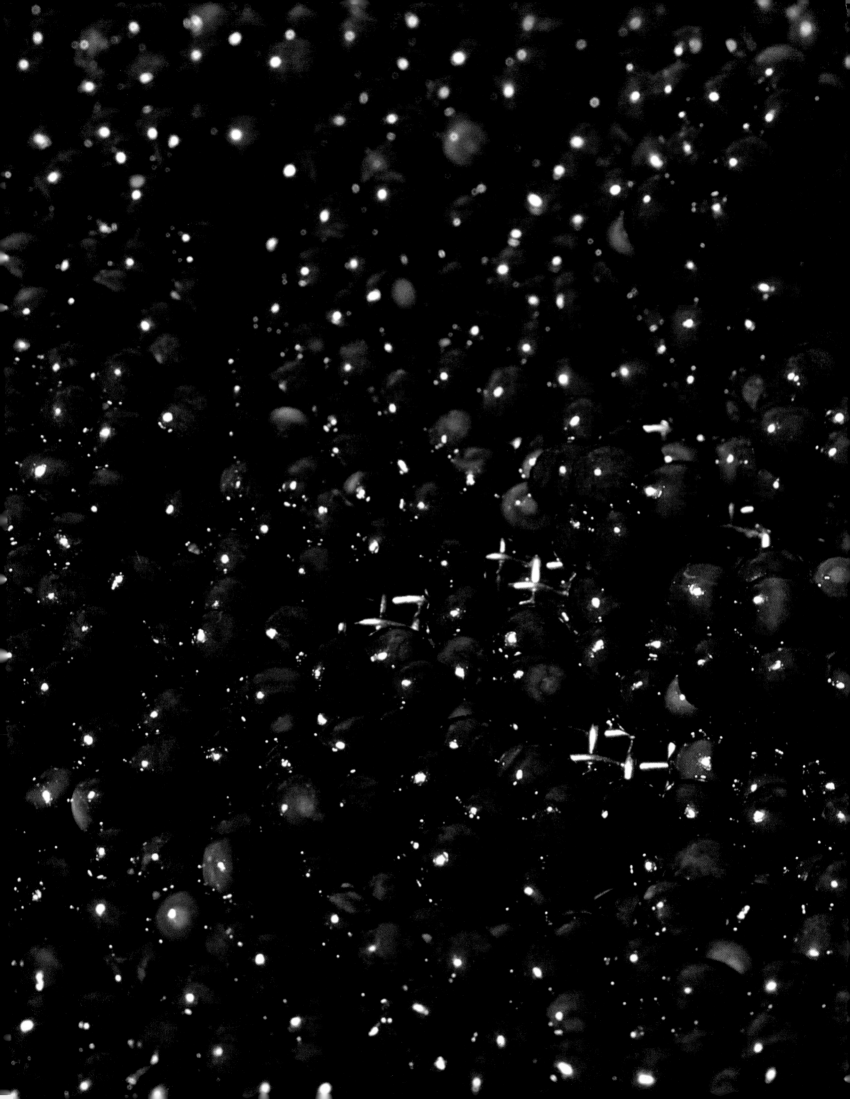

Harvesting the eggs

Extracting
the roe

The small wooden cabins and sheds where caviar used to be produced are long gone; they have since been replaced by austere buildings that resemble pharmaceutical laboratories more than anything else—a consequence of the industrialization of caviar production, which must meet a constantly increasing demand as well as extremely strict standards of quality and hygiene.

From the docks, the sturgeon is placed on a metal conveyor or is hauled uphill to the processing plant, where it is placed on a metal table and white-jacketed specialists take over from the fishermen. The first step is to wash the fish with fresh water, then make an incision in the belly of the female while she is still alive to remove and weigh the roe as quickly as possible. Iranian fishermen receive a bonus in pay, depending on the weight of the fish.

The female sturgeon is merely stunned before being cut open.

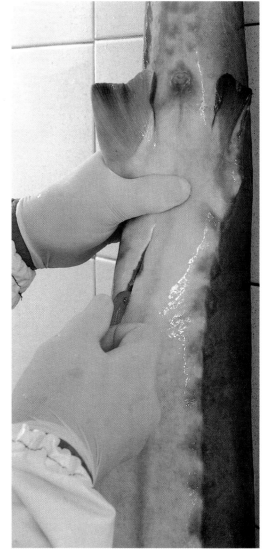

The incision is a delicate operation that must be done precisely and quickly.

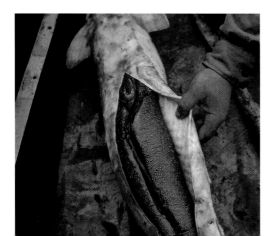

Once the fish is dead, its body releases a chemical substance that is harmful to the eggs.

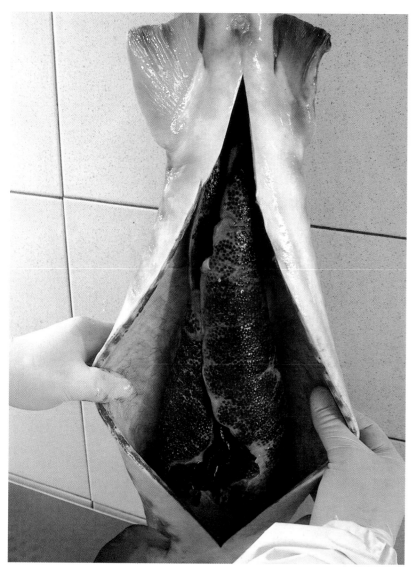

Once extracted from the fish, the roe is carefully weighed and placed in a receptacle prior to processing.

The eggs are held together by a membrane that must be removed before they are considered edible.

Work conditions were once much more precarious than they are today, and the fish often were cut open right on the loading docks. Astrakhan, circa 1930.

Washing
and filtering the eggs

Opposite page and below: The sorting and filtering is a very delicate operation, as too much pressure may damage the eggs.

The caviar is placed on a sieve that has holes varying from 2 to 4 millimeters across, immediately after they have been weighed. This operation separates the eggs from the sack. Earlier, birch branches were used to whip the eggs, although this had the unfortunate consequence of damaging a large number of them. After this first sorting step, the grains are washed again then placed on a horsehair sieve.

Next, they are classified, a decisive step in the preparation. The firmness of the eggs, the color, size, smell and taste of the grains are taken into account. Depending on these various criteria, the master blender decides which eggs will be used to make first- or second-class caviar, fresh caviar, pressed caviar or pasteurized caviar.

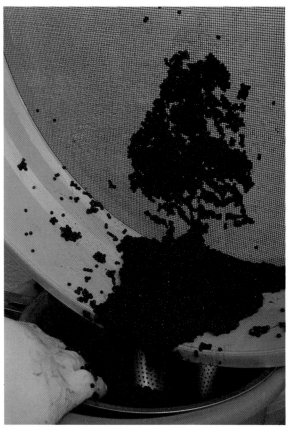

The caviar is placed in a sieve to separate the eggs from the sack.

The eggs must be prepared according to very stringent hygiene standards to ensure proper storage.

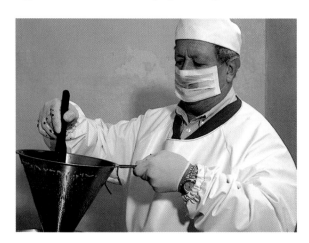

The sorting and filtering used to take place directly on the docks. U.S.S.R. circa 1925.

Washing and filtering the eggs on the wharf in the Astrahkan region, circa 1930.

The eggs are cleaned during each step in processing to eliminate all residue and impurities.

Salting
the eggs

After the caviar is salted, the precious pearls are drained once last time to get rid of excess brine prior to packaging.

O nce the caviar has been sorted and classified, it is weighed again and the master salt blender decides how to salt the eggs. The finest caviar is called "malossol," and has from 2.8 to 4 percent of salt by weight. Caviar with a low salt content generally contains borax, which is an illegal food additive in the United States. In the U.S., therefore, caviar has a higher salt content to compensate for the lack of a preserving agent. The quantity of salt can be from 6 to 10 percent by weight. As the salt is added, the caviar is stirred to salt evenly. This must be done quickly as good-quality caviar must remain firm and if it is overstirred, it becomes sticky.

The quantity of salt added is obviously of utmost importance. In the past, the Russian master salt blenders had an intuitive understanding of the process. They gathered their salt from the seas of the Russian Steppe; this salt was stored in a dry room for seven years to remove the excess chlorine.

The eggs are constantly weighed throughout the caviar-making process. Precision is essential in ensuring the quality of the product.

Caviar is not fit for consumption before it is salted. Salt preserves it and gives it flavor.

The Russian master salt blenders were highly reputed for their fine-quality salt.

Prior to salting, the eggs are carefully sorted and classified.

Certain salts were known for their refinement and purity, such as the highly reputed salt from Lüneberg, Germany.

Packaging
the caviar

After it has been salted, the caviar is then spread on a very fine mesh in order to remove the brine, or excess liquid, absorbed by the salt. The eggs lose from 5 to 6 percent of their weight during this process. The eggs are then carefully placed on a platter in order to be canned; from here, the eggs are packed into lacquer-coated metal tins, which helps to preserve them. When capped, these metal tins are airtight.

The boxes must be filled quite rapidly, so that the caviar does not settle. The boxes must also be filled right up to the brim, leaving a minimum amount of air in the tin to prevent mold. The boxes are quickly hand-packed using a small wooden spatula. To avoid moisture, a small amount of air must remain in the box. Once the cover of the tin has been capped on tightly, and the excess liquid and air removed, the famous elastic bands seal the containers, making them airtight.

The tins used for export generally weigh approximately 4 lbs; they are shipped and then repackaged by retailers once they reach the final market. The type of packaging described here corresponds to the "malossol" quality caviar. Other types of packaging exist for other categories of caviar, such as glass jars, which are used primarily for pasteurized caviar and oak or linden-tree barrels, which are used in packaging salted caviar.

The classic metal tin with the cap dating from the last century is still the number one choice in packaging.

The packaging must be done rapidly and skillfully to avoid damaging the eggs.

The tins must be filled right to the brim, leaving a minimum amount of air in the tin to prevent mold.

Caviar experts can judge the quality of caviar merely by its appearance.

The eggs are now processed in buildings that resemble pharmaceutical laboratories.

The larger 4 lbs boxes are better for shipping caviar. Retailers then repackage the caviar in smaller tins once it reaches the final market.

The box's cap makes the tin airtight and gives the caviar its smooth surface when the tin is opened.

The ritual steps, as carried out by a Russian caviar-producer near Astrakhan in the 1930s.

The boxes are quickly hand-packed using a small wooden spatula, which does not alter the taste of the eggs. Great strides in progress have been made in terms of hygiene and quality.

The famous elastic bands seal the containers, making them airtight.

Transportation

O nce the caviar has been packed, it must be sent to the final customer; this often involves long distances and travel can be disastrous for caviar if it is not properly protected.

Through the late 1970s, the metal tins of malossol caviar and pressed caviar were placed in square wooden boxes, which were then set in large refrigerated barrels that contained fifty-four 4 lbs tins. The barrels were lined with woven reeds to insulate the caviar. The boxes were generally wrapped in packets of three in canvas bags sealed in Iran. The entire batch of caviar was then shipped by boat from Leningrad to various destinations.

More modern transport and refrigeration facilities have made it possible to send caviar by refrigerated truck directly from the Caspian Sea.

Barrels that were once used in shipping caviar had to be thoroughly cleaned before being used again. Astrakhan, circa 1930.

The 4 lbs tins were wrapped in packets of three and numbered before being shipped in barrels. The packets were separated by wooden inserts to insulate them.

Once the barrels were sealed,
they were rolled toward
the boats that transported
them to Europe.
Astrakhan, circa 1930.

As boats were not
equipped with refrigeration
systems in the early part
of the century, ice was placed
in the barrels.

Sturgeon meat

Opposite page: On the island of Gyzylsuw, located two hours by boat from Turkmenbasby, Turkmenistan, sturgeon filets dry in the summer sun and are consumed the following winter.

Sturgeon are not fished only for their eggs, even if caviar remains their most famous product. The flesh of the fish is particularly tasty and resembles white meat. It was once highly prized by royalty, and a number of recipes can be found in ancient texts describing the preparation of this mythical fish. Today, fresh sturgeon is rarely found on the market, but it is possible to find smoked filets in a few specialty shops. Fleshy pieces from the back of the fish, weighing 2lbs and 3 oz to 4 lbs and 6 oz , are precooked to facilitate the pickling process, then smoked. Sturgeon filet should be served cool but not cold, much like a salmon filet, and it is particularly recommended for diabetics.

Although fresh sturgeon is rarely found on the market, the flesh is particularly tasty and delicate.

Like salt, the sun has been used to preserved food since Antiquity. Here, sturgeon filets are being sun-dried.

Fleshy pieces from the fish are removed (above), dried and salted (right), and eaten the following winter.

Varieties of caviar

Beluga,
Osetra and Sevruga

Taken from the *Huso huso*, the largest of the sturgeon species, beluga caviar has the largest grain. An average 33 lbs of eggs are taken from each fish, and the color varies from light to dark gray, depending on the size of the eggs. They are generally larger than the other types and are therefore more fragile. Considered to be the finest available, the beluga is the most expensive caviar, although gourmets do not all agree that it is the best. Produced in the Astrakhan region, beluga was virtually the only caviar that was known in the West in the early twentieth century, as the other caviar-producing regions were far too remote for optimal transport conditions. Once refrigerated warehouses were constructed around the Kura and the Anzali, other types of caviars gradually began to appear on the market and Beluga progressively lost its exclusive position with respect to the other various types of caviar.

Osetra, from the *Acipenser gueldenstaedti*, has smaller grains and is firmer than beluga caviar. It is also less perishable. Females produce from five to twenty kilograms of eggs. Osetra caviar ranges in color from dark brown to gold, and sometimes slate gray. It has a distinct, almost nutty taste, and many connoisseurs consider this to be the best caviar.

Sevruga, from the *Acipenser stellatus*, is the smallest-grained caviar. Some two to eight kilograms of eggs are produced by the female sturgeon. The eggs are dark gray in color and have a strong taste of iodine. The eggs are so delicate that they burst open quickly when eaten, releasing their fine flavor. Sevruga costs far less than osetra and beluga caviar, as it is more plentiful and has a smaller grain.

A variety of sizes to suit everyone's taste and budget.

The different varieties of caviar are often color-coded.

Sevruga is the smallest-grained and least expensive of the three varieties, but it has the strongest flavor.

Sampling all three types of caviar at the same time gives a better idea of their differences.

From Malossol
to pressed caviar

The quality of caviar obviously depends on the origin and the type of preparation, as well as the care taken during the preparation stage.

Connoisseurs prefer fresh malossol, which contains a maximum of 5 percent salt by weight. Borax, which acts as a preservative, is added in France to caviar with low salt content (not in the United States, however, where borax is an illegal food additive). Caviar processed with borax can be kept for up to one year, although it is preferable to eat it within six months after it has been packaged. Major caviar consumers are also advised against purchasing large, 9 ozs or 1 lbs and 2 ozs tins that do not come in their original boxes, and this is for reasons of conservation.

In addition, specialists read the information printed on the side of the tin when the caviar was packed. This indicates the number of fish, the number of tins filled with roe from the same fish, and the color classification of the caviar (light, medium, dark). If the tin is to be kept for a certain amount of time, consumers are also advised to turn it over regularly so that the oil is evenly distributed and to prevent brine from forming.

The second quality found on the market is salted caviar, which contains up to 8 percent of salt by weight. This type of caviar is generally destined for the American market, where borax is prohibited by law.

The third quality is pressed caviar, made from soft, broken or overmature eggs. They are placed in a highly salted, hot brine and shaken until the caviar is no longer milky. This salted caviar is then placed in cheesecloth and put in small oak barrels coated with paraffin. The caviar is then pressed to remove the excess liquid. This type of caviar used to

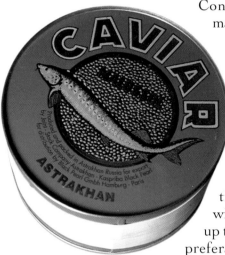

The finest caviar is called "malossol," meaning "little salt," and has 5 percent of salt by weight.

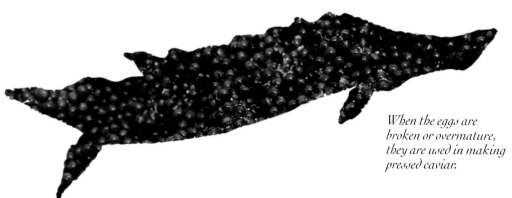

When the eggs are broken or overmature, they are used in making pressed caviar.

Borax is added to malossol and acts as a preservative. This crystalline compound used to be present in salt collected around the Caspian.

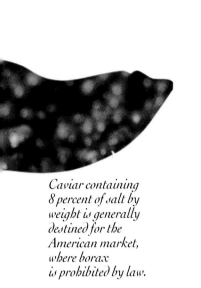

Caviar containing 8 percent of salt by weight is generally destined for the American market, where borax is prohibited by law.

be so thick that it could be sliced with a knife, but pressed caviar today is softer and can be spread like jam. Russians prefer the strong flavor of this caviar, which is also recommended for cooking. Finally, the last quality is pasteurized caviar: it is vacuum-packed in small glass jars three to four hours after the fish has reached the processing plant. The pasteurization process, which involves heating the eggs, alters the flavor of the caviar, but it can then be stored for a longer period of time.

Engraving depicting Easter festivities in Russia.

Some producers pasteurize caviar; it is vacuum-packed in small glass jars. This alters the flavor of the caviar, but it can be stored for longer periods of time.

What Brands should you choose?

Contrary to what is commonly believed, Volga brand caviar is actually French. It was founded by Robert de Lalagade in 1923.

Choosing a brand name caviar is a guarantee of quality; it often also means paying a higher price, but the consumer can be assured of the best harvesting, processing and transportation techniques, and therefore a finer product.

In Russia in the early twentieth century, the caviar market was controlled by three families: the Sapochnikov in the Astrakhan region; the Vorobiov in the province of Saint Petersburg; and the Lazar Mailov & Sons company in the Baku region. This last company built innovative refrigerated warehouses at the turn of the century that are still in working order; the Azerbaijan government plans to transform them into a museum in the near future.

In France during this same period, a single fish merchant by the name of Émile Prunier was importing small quantities of caviar that he sold to a few connoisseurs. It took the Russian revolution, and the flight of two brothers, Melkom and Mougcheg Petrossian, from the country for the caviar industry to take off in the West. Students at the time, they decided that the time—Paris in the Roaring Twenties—was ripe to launch the black pearls. One of the two brothers married a daughter of the Mailov family, cementing the link between Paris and the caviar-producing regions. The brothers gambled on the staying power of the new regime in Russia and negotiated a monopoly on caviar exports to France with the new Minister of Foreign Commerce for the Soviet

Kaspia brand caviar was launched in 1927. Two years later, the shop on Place de la Madeleine in Paris opened.

Choosing a brand name caviar is a guarantee of quality and often means paying a higher price.

The Petrossian brothers were the ones who were instrumental in launching caviar in France in the 1920s.

Dom Petroff is a brand launched by the Petrossian company.

Each variety of the delicious black pearls has its own label, packaging and color.

The proud silhouette of the Petrossian rigged merchant ship cuts a swathe through much of the world-wide caviar market.

These 4 lbs tins are for professionals. The black pearls runneth over...

Some brands, such as Caviar House, use a variety of colored tins to differentiate various types and quality of caviar.

What Brands
should you choose?

Republics. The early years were difficult, however, and at the 1920 Gastronomic Exhibition in the Grand Palais in Paris, the Petrossians had to install spittoons around their stand—tasting was free, but few people appreciated this new product.

Yet Petrossian is not the only caviar-producer; other highly reputed brands include Dieckmann & Hansen, one of the oldest German companies; the Caviar House in Switzerland and Great Britain; Kaspia in France; Volga in France; Porimex in Switzerland; and W. G. White Ltd. in Great Britain.

Caviar d'Aquitaine, a relative newcomer on the market, is produced from sturgeon raised on freshwater farms.

A beautiful ceramic box dating from the nineteenth century used in packaging Kaspia caviar.

The 4 lbs boxes of Iranian caviar are identical, but each one is marked with specific references giving information on the catch.

Iranian caviar is packaged by the state-run company SHILAT before it is sold to foreign distributors, who then repackage the caviar in its own tins.

Tins of Russian caviar in Astrakhan, circa 1930.

The Russian boxes are inspired by the bright colors of such traditional handicraft as the Matryoshka dolls.

Filtering salmon
eggs. The various
stages in producing
keta caviar
are identical to
those for sturgeon.

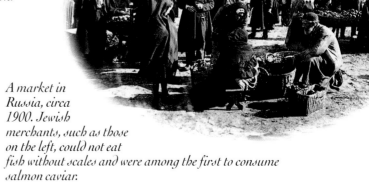

A market in
Russia, circa
1900. Jewish
merchants, such as those
on the left, could not eat
fish without scales and were among the first to consume
salmon caviar.

Imitation pearls

Lefthand page: Female eskimos in the far eastern regions of Russia extract eggs from salmon to make red caviar.

Caviar, as a luxury product, has been imitated often, by products that are similar to the real thing in name only. By law, the word "caviar" alone cannot be placed on a label for anything other than sturgeon eggs. Other fish roe must be qualified with the name of the fish: salmon, lumpfish and so on.

The earliest imitations of caviar were probably made from salmon eggs and were produced around the Black Sea by Jews who were not allowed to eat the eggs of the sturgeon, as the fish does not have scales. Prepared in a similar way to real caviar, "red caviar," which is also known as "keta caviar," is fairly refined in taste and is slightly more perishable than sturgeon eggs. Red caviar became more and more popular in Europe beginning in the eighteenth century, and remains so today. It is produced in Russia, America and Finland, which has recently started exporting large quantities to Japan.

Danish caviar, which is made from lumpfish, has acquired a large share of the market and often replaces keta caviar. Danish caviar can be stored for long periods of time, is easy to process, and can stand large quantities of salt, all of which facilitates transportation. Coloring agents are also generally added. It obviously cannot be compared in taste to real caviar, as it retains a strong fishy flavor.

A third natural product has recently appeared as a competitor to real caviar. This is "trout caviar," produced from sea trout roe, which is sometimes colored black. Some producers have no scruples about labeling it "black malossol," in an attempt to create confusion between this product and authentic caviar. These eggs, whether or not they are colored, taste something like keta caviar.

This list would be incomplete without mentioning one of the oldest preparations made from fish eggs: *boutargue.* Made from dried mullet roe, this was a highly prized dish among the Greeks and

Danish caviar is made from much smaller, firmer lumpfish roe. It has a strong fishy taste.

Salmon eggs are more fragile than sturgeon eggs. They have a somewhat refined taste, but are much less flavorful.

Righthand page :
keta caviar may
not be as refined
as authentic
caviar, but it is
still considered
something of a
luxury product.

*I*mitation
pearls

*Artificial coloring
is sometimes
added to lumpfish
roe to make it look
more like caviar.*

Romans, and it is still carried by certain specialty shops. Because of its appearance and its price, it cannot be mistaken for caviar.

Entirely new products have recently appeared; they are all somewhat artificial and are intended for a larger public. Spain, Russia, Japan and Israel are large producers of this type of product. Spain, for example, sells a product called Eurocaviar, which is made from mullet, herring and salmon roe. The product has a high natural resistance to hot and cold temperatures and is therefore very good for cooking purposes. Russia, however, produces a protein caviar that contains no fish whatsoever — it is made from casein, egg yolk, gelatin, tannin, coloring agents and artificial flavorings. The texture and color are surprisingly good, but from a nutritional and gourmet point of view, it is worthless.

An identification system has been created in an attempt to counteract this invasion of imitations and to distinguish true caviar from the rest. It uses an isoelectric convergence to determine the species from which an egg comes, by isolating the protein and creating a spectrum for each type of sturgeon and other fish.

Someone looking for a good caviar, however, is advised to purchase from reputable caviar dealers. The prices may be slightly higher, but a good brand name is a guarantee of quality.

*An ersatz caviar
cocktail
of lumpfish and
salmon roe.*

Very precise scientific procedures are used in detecting counterfeits.

Regulations in France are very strict, and all products labeled caviar must come from the sturgeon.

Savoring caviar

Is *Caviar* nutritious?

Specialists have always claimed that caviar has many virtues. In his *Grand Dictionnaire de cuisine,* Dumas indicated that Kaviar, made from «salted sturgeon eggs… has the property of preparing the stomach for other food, and can therefore replace soup.» Brillat-Savarin, in his

Physiologie du goût, discussed the effects of an fish diet: «unanimous observations have demonstrated that it acts strongly on genetics, and awakens in both sexes the instinct of reproduction.»
With 270 calories per 100 grams, caviar is not a high-calory food. It is, however, rich in protein (25.3 grams per 100 grams), fat (17 gr per 100 gr) and cholesterol (440 mg per 100 gr), but is low in sugar (4 gr per 100 gr). It also has a high content of mineral salts: 1,700 mg sodium, 164 mg potassium, 330 mg phosphorus and 51 mg calcium, along with vitamins D, A, C, B2, B44, B12 and PP. The recommended portion is from 30 to 50 gr of caviar per person.

Caviar should be served with a suitable utensil of gold, wood or horn, never silver, which alters the taste of the caviar. The best way to fully appreciate caviar is to taste small quantities, letting the grains burst open in the mouth to release their delicate flavor. All accompaniments pepper, lemon, onion and herbs must be banished from the table. Those who find the taste of caviar too strong are advised to spread a small amount on a blini or sliced bread. But the true connoisseur always prefers to eat caviar unadorned. According to Russian tradition, white vodka is the perfect accompaniment, but caviar is also delicious with dry champagne. Many chefs have recently created innovated recipes that incorporate caviar into complex dishes in the best of them, the delicate flavor is brought out by the contrasting interplay of flavors.

Caviar is ideal for keeping fit.

Caviar is highly rich in nutrients, vitamins and minerals and does not have to be served in large quantities.

How to Taste caviar?

The bland taste of blinis is perfect for caviar's delicate flavor.

Caviar is an exceptional food item served for special occasions, such as New Year's Eve in Saint Petersburg.

Tasting must be done with the appropriate cutlery, either made of horn, wood or gold, rather than silver, which would irremedialbly alter the taste of the caviar. Its basic flavor evokes egg yolk, embellished with a touch of herb and iodine, and even, according to the variety, of hazelnut. The smell of caviar, which also has its importance, is very typical and will be soft and fresh if it is a quality product.

The best way to enjoy caviar is to proceed in small quantities set down on the tongue, letting the grains burst on the palate to deliver their delicate flavors. All along its long history, it was given accompaniments such as pepper, lemon, onions and herbs which are definitely to be banned. For those who may consider the first taste of caviar to be too strong, it is recommended to have it with a neutral complement such as a slice of white bread or a blini, a kind of small russian pancake made of risen dough.

Sampling several varieties of caviar in one sitting is the ultimate in luxury and allows taste comparisons.

Righthand page: Sometimes a dollop of cream is served on the blini and can temper the taste of caviar if it is too strong.

Pure-grain vodkas and their neutral taste do not mask the full flavor of caviar.

Sturgeon fishermen enjoy caviar with a minimum of accoutrements.

How to Taste caviar?

The connoisseur will always prefer a plain tasting, keeping his attention to the magical fragrances of the precious little black grains. Recently, numerous chefs have innovated by associating caviar to some complex recipes, where the taste of the priceless black pearl, far from being buried under other ingredients, is enhanced by the set of contrasting flavors.

The tiny spoon is the choice implement of caviar aficionados.

Chic restaurants always have a few tins of caviar stashed away for exclusive customers.

Osetra caviar, with it subtle nutty taste, is served here in a glass bowl over ice with a flat spoon.

Selected

cases...

The sensual experience of sampling caviar is reflected in this voluptuously sculpted spoon.

An exceptional dish for celebration, caviar must be tasted according to precise rules if one wants to appreciate all its flavorful qualities; the whole protocol must be respected to enjoy this sea jewel. Before anything else, care must be given to take the box out of the refrigerator (where it is kept between 36 and 39° F) at least fifteen minutes before the meal, for the aromas to reconstitute. In order to avoid reheating, which could be disastrous to its taste, it is preferable to encircle the original box (from which it will be served) in crushed ice.

This Iranian serving dish in chased silver provides a spectacular way of serving caviar and keeping it at the right temperature.

An elegant old-fashioned vodka bottle and vodka shot glass with a chased silver base dating from the eighteenth century accompanied the finest caviar.

Let the imagination run wild in serving this marvelous product.

A tradition table laden with Russian specialties from the early twentieth century, including a samovar and vodka. The tin of caviar is accorded a prominent position.

Two small plates dating from the eighteenth century. The size of the serving dishes must be considered, given the small proportions of caviar that are served.

The greatest glassmakers have created fine pieces for serving caviar. This one is by Lalique.

Glass receptacles do not alter the taste of caviar.

Selected
cases...

*Opposite page:
A refined way of
serving Dom
Petroff caviar on
an icy bed with
two small shots of
frozen vodka.*

Even though their use is tempting, ancient plates made of engraved metal may alter the taste of the product. If one insists on using one, however, one should choose a glass or porcelain plate.

The problem encountered for the presentation of caviar is that it is tasted in small quantities and seems lost in the middle of a large plate. That is why some manufacturers have tried to remedy this by proposing individual display units, allowing the pearl of kings to keep all of its prestige until the end of the tasting.

Silversmiths have created elaborate glasses for drinking vodka.

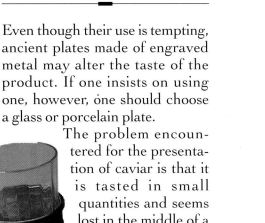

A great number of kinds of vodka has always existed in Russia. Some bottles are displayed in silver tripods to underscore their prestige.

Ice keeps the grains at the right temperature.

Vodka is best served chilled.

Caviar is synonymous with festivities and warm, plush settings.

Displaying caviar in a raised serving dish allows everyone to admire the black pearls.

Recipes

Oyster purses with fresh salmon and Osetra caviar

Ingredients

24 medium-sized oysters
12 ounces of fresh salmon filet, cut into 24 flat, square slices
6 tablespoons unsalted butter
1/2 pound fresh spinach leaves
juice of one lemon
2 tablespoons thick cream
1/2 ounce Osetra caviar
1 bunch of chives
salt and white pepper

4 OR 8 PEOPLE
PREPARATION: 1 HOUR
COOKING TIME: 1 MINUTE

Preheat the oven to 350° F (180° C). Open the oysters and remove them from their shells. Save and strain the liquid from the oysters.

Drain the oysters in a piece of cheesecloth.

Place a square slice of salmon on a sheet of plastic wrap. Set one oyster in the middle. Pull up the edges of the plastic wrap toward the center to form a purse shape, then roll over to seal. Remove from the plastic and place in a buttered dish. Prepare the remaining oysters and salmon purses in the same way. Add pepper and set aside.

Remove the stems from the spinach and wash thoroughly. Drain the spinach. Heat a non-stick pan. When hot, add the spinach leaves for several seconds.

Pour the oyster liquid into a saucepan. Bring to a boil, then simmer until the liquid has almost completely evaporated.

Add the lemon juice, cream and remaining butter (cut into small pieces). Stir until the sauce is smooth.

Place the salmon purses in the oven for one minute to cook the salmon slightly.

Arrange the spinach on each plate. Place 3 or 6 salmon purses in the center, then add a spoonful of sauce.

Garnish with the caviar and few sprigs of chive. Serve immediately.

Sturgeon-stuffed cabbage with caviar sauce

Ingredients

1 small green cabbage
1 cup fish broth
7 tablespoons unsalted butter
2 ounces chopped smoked sturgeon
1 large shallot, minced
1/2 cup white wine
1/2 cup fish bouillon
1 1/2 cup crème fraiche
1 ounce smoked herring
2 ounces caviar
1 ounce salmon roe
12 large Brussels sprout leaves
salt and pepper

4 PEOPLE

PREPARATION:
40 MINUTES

COOKING TIME:
10 MINUTES

Remove leaves from the cabbage. Blanch them in salted boiling water for 5 minutes. Plunge immediately in cold water, drain and remove any stalky sections. Set aside 4 leaves and chop up the others.

Heat the fish broth. Cut 6 tablespoons of butter into small pieces and add to the broth. Add the whole and chopped cabbage leaves to the liquid and simmer for 5 minutes. Drain.

Mix the sturgeon and chopped cabbage. Spread out the four large cabbage leaves and place the stuffing in the center. Fold in each leaf to form four rolls, each about 2 inches across. Set aside.

Place the wine in a saucepan, bring to a simmer and add the shallots. Add the fish bouillon.

Bring to a boil, add the crème fraiche and let simmer. Add the herring. Add salt and pepper to taste. Set aside and keep warm.

Heat up the caviar and salmon roe in a double boiler. Blanch the Brussels sprout leaves in salted boiling water for several minutes. Let them cool down, drain and sauté them lightly in a pan with the remaining 1 tablespoon butter. Steam the stuffed cabbages to reheat. Cut into quarters to the base and arrange on individual plates. Arrange the Brussels sprout leaves and garnish with the caviar.

Pour a small ring of sauce around each cabbage and carefully arrange the salmon roe between the sauce and the cabbage. Serve immediately.

131

Small mackerel filets
with horseradish and caviar sauce

Ingredients

6 small mackerel, cleaned, and with heads and fins removed.
1 tablespoon olive oil
3/4 cup seeded, chopped cucumber
2 large tomatoes
6 mint leaves
6 basil leaves
1/3 cup balsamic vinegar
2 ounces caviar
1 sprig of dill, salt

Horseradish

1 tablespoon chopped horseradish
2 tablespoons thick cream
1 tablespoon sherry vinegar
3/4 cup mayonnaise
salt and pepper

Preheat the over to 400° F. Wash the fish, remove the filets and pat dry. Cut off the edges to remove any remaining bones. Cut each filet in half lengthwise. Set aside. Oil six 2 1/2-inch ring molds.
Slice the cucumber into 2-inch sections. Remove the seeds and chop the remaining cucumber into small cubes. Then blanch in boiling salted water for several minutes. Run under cold water and drain. Cut the tomatoes into quarters, remove the seeds and chop into small pieces. Add to cucumber. Cut up the mint and basil leaves. Set aside.
To prepare the sauce: add the grated horseradish, crème fraiche and vinegar to the mayonnaise. Add salt and pepper. Blend well and strain. Add half of the sauce to the tomato and cucumber mixture. Add the mint and basil and mix gently. Set aside the remaining sauce.
Line each ring mold with 4 mackerel filets, skin side facing outward. Arrange the ring molds on a baking dish and cook for 3 to 4 minutes. Remove the molds and deglaze with a few drops of vinegar. Remove the ring molds.
Fill the molded fish filets with the tomato and cucumber mixture. Line the bottom of each plate with the horseradish sauce. Simmer the remaining vinegar until it has thickened into a syrup. Place in a pastry bag and garnish around the sauce with small drops of sauce. using a toothpick, draw a line between the drops to create an attractive design. Using a spatula, carefully arrange the fish in the center of each plate. Place a dollop of caviar on the tomato and cucumber mixture and garnish with some fresh dill. Serve immediately.

6 PEOPLE
PREPARATION: 40 MINUTES
COOKING TIME: 3 TO 4 MINUTES

Sardine butterflies with
mustard cream and Sevruga caviar sauce

Ingredients
18 whole, fresh sardines
2 tablespoons coarse salt
1/3 cup olive oil
juice of 2 lemons
1 teaspoon dry mustard
1/4 cup dry white wine
1 cup crème fraiche
1 bunch of chives
6 ounces Sevruga caviar
salt and pepper

Remove the heads from the sardines and filet them by slicing along the backbone from the head to the tail. Wash the filets and pat dry. Trim the skin and remove any bones.

Cut the filets in half and arrange them in a dish. Sprinkle with the coarse salt and let sit, refrigerated, for 1 hour. Then rinse the sardine filets under cold water, pat dry and place in a flat dish.

Set aside a few drops of lemon juice and blend the remaining juice with the oil. Pour this sauce over the sardine filets, add freshly ground pepper and let marinate for 1 hour.

Prepare the cream sauce: Dissolve the mustard in the wine and add the remaining drops of lemon juice. Add salt and pepper to taste. Add the crème fraiche and 1 teaspoon of chopped chives. Whip the cream mixture. Gently fold in 2 ounces of caviar.

Place a spoonful of caviar cream in the center of each plate.

Arrange 6 half-filets on either side of the cream.

Complete the "butterflies" by arranging 2 strands of chives as antennae and decorating with 1 ounce of caviar at the tips of each filet.

6 PEOPLE

PREPARATION: 25 MINUTES

MARINATE FOR 2 HOURS.

Braised veal
with caviar sauce

Ingredients

4 pounds deboned veal shank
1 lemon
2 tablespoons butter
3 onions, chopped
1 carrot, chopped
1 clove
3 bay leaves
1 bouquet garni
1 tablespoon oil
1 cup dry white wine
3 ounces caviar
salt and pepper

8 PEOPLE

PREPARATION:
25 MINUTES

COOKING TIME:
90 MINUTES

Grate and chop the lemon peel. Squeeze the juice and set aside. Melt the butter in a saucepan. Add the vegetables, clove, bay leaves, bouquet garni and lemon peel. Sauté for 15 minutes, but don't let the vegetables brown.

Preheat the oven to 300° F.

Heat the oil in a frying pan and brown the veal. Add salt and pepper. Place the veal in the saucepan, on top of the sauted vegetables, add the wine and braise in the oven for 90 minutes.

Remove the meat from the saucepan and keep warm. Strain the cooking juices. Simmer the sauce for several minutes, add the caviar, stirring gently, then add the lemon juice.

Just before serving, cut the veal in thin slices, arrange in a serving platter and pour the caviar sauce over it.

Potato cakes with bacon and caviar

6 PEOPLE

PREPARATION: 45 MINUTES

COOKING TIME: 20 MINUTES

Ingredients
3 pounds small new potatoes
2 pounds butter
26 slices of bacon
2 large onions
2 shallots
2 cups dry white wine
1 cup cream
4 ounces Sevruga caviar
4 strands of chive
salt and pepper

P eel and wash the potatoes. Slice thinly. Cover with water and set aside.
Cut the butter into small pieces, place them in a thick-bottomed saucepan over low heat to melt. Skim off the foam, then carefully pour the melted butter into another bowl. Set aside and keep warm. Cut a circle of wax paper to fit the bottom of 6 individual tart pans, then arrange 6 pieces of bacon in each one so that the ends stick over the edges. Place the pans in the refrigerator. Peel and chop the onions.

Sauté them gently in the clarified butter for a few minutes. Set aside. Strain and pat dry the sliced potatoes. Poach them in the hot clarified butter for 4 minutes, then drain.
Preheat oven to 360° F.
To assemble to potato cakes: remove the tart pans from the refrigerator. Arrange one layer of potatoes in each pan and place one spoonful of onions in the center. Add another layer of potatoes, then fold the bacon slices back toward the center, covering the potatoes. Place in the oven and bake for 20 minutes.

Meanwhile, peel and chop the shallots. Place them in a saucepan, add the wine and simmer until 1 tablespoon of liquid remains. Add the crème fraiche. Simmer for 5 minutes, until the sauce thickens slightly. Salt and pepper to taste. Strain and set aside. Remove the pans from the ovens and place the potato cakes on individual dinner plates. Carefully arrange a spoonful of caviar on each cake. Surround with a bead of sauce. Garnish with the chives and serve immediately.

Eggs with caviar

6 PEOPLE

PREPARATION: 30 MINUTES

COOKING TIME: 3 TO 4 MINUTES

Ingredients
6 eggs
cayenne pepper
5 tablespoons butter
2 ounces caviar
1/2 cup cream
2 tablespoons vodka
juice of 1/4 lemon
salt

C arefully remove the top of each eggshell. Place the eggs in a bowl and set aside the shells. Add salt and cayenne pepper. Beat for 1 to 2 minutes, then place bowl over a double boiler. When the mixture starts to thicken, add the butter in small pieces, mixing with a wooden spoon.
Return the mixture to the empty egg shells.
Whip the cream; add the vodka and lemon juice, mixing gently. Fill a pastry bag with this mixture and decorate the top of the eggs. Add 1/2 ounce of caviar to each and serve immediately.

Cabbage rolls with salmon and caviar

12 ROLLS

PREPARATION: 15 MINUTES

COOKING TIME: 3 TO
4 MINUTES

Ingredients
3 green cabbage leaves
1/4 pound smoked salmon
1 ounce Sevruga caviar
salt

Blanch the cabbage leaves in salted boiling water for 3 to 4 minutes. Rinse under cold water and drain. pat dry, remove the ribs and cut our four squares, 5 1/2 inches on a side.
Cut the smoked salmon into 4 slices and arrange each one on a cabbage leaf. Roll each leaf up into a cigar shape and wrap with plastic film. Refrigerate. Just before serving, remove the plastic wrap and cut each cabbage roll into four 1-inch sections. Place each section vertically on a plate and place a bit of caviar on each one.

Cold taglierini salad with caviar

4 PEOPLE

PREPARATION:
15 MINUTES

COOKING TIME: 4 TO
5 MINUTES

Ingredients
3 ounces thin taglierini
2 tablespoons olive oil
1 bunch of chives
2 ounces caviar
1 teaspoon chopped shallots
salt

Cook the taglierini in salted boiling water until done. Run the pasta under cold water and drain.
Add olive oil and mix gently.
Arrange the pasta in dinner plates.
Sprinkle with chopped chives.
Place 1/5 ounce of caviar in the center of each plate. Add the shallots and serve immediately.

Index

Page numbers in italics refer to photographs

Photographic credits

Acknowledgements

We would like to thank Mr Armen Petrossian from Petrossian and Professor Billard,
of the Ichtyology Laboratory at the Natural History Museum for their advice.
Many thanks to Kaspia, a restaurant on Place de la Madeleine in Paris,
who allowed us to photograph on their premises.

Captions for chapter headings and two page spreads

p. 4: Beluga caviar; pp. 6-7: Sign for a caviar production center on the Caspain Sea;
pp. 16-17: Fishing sturgeon with nets in the early 20th century.; pp. 22-23: A 60-pound sturgeon caught in the Rhone River;
pp. 30-31: Sturgeon fishing at the mouth of the Volga River; pp. 34-35: Aerial view of the Volga delta;
pp. 44-45: A caviar production plant in Iran; pp. 50-51: An old fisherman, Nicholay Bogdan, on the Volga;
pp. 54-55: The Yangtze River in China; pp. 60-61: Sturgeon fishing in the Saint Laurence River in Canada (1958);
pp. 64-65: Setting nets for sturgeon fishing in Atyrau, Kazakhstan; p. 70: Sturgeon on conveyor belts are transported to the processing plant;
p. 71: Fishermen on the Volga; p. 76: A sturgeon is cut open in; p. 77: Net fishing in the Volga; pp. 80-81: Close-up view of caviar;
p. 84: Caviar packing in Russia; p. 85: Extracting the roe from the sturgeon in Russia ;
pp. 94-95: Sturgeon meat drying on Gyzylsuw Island in Turkmenistan ; pp. 98-99: The different varieties of caviar;
pp. 112-113: A table at the Kaspia restaurant; pp. 124-125: Caviar tasting in Russia;
pp. 126-127: Salmon and fennel with oyster caviar cream.

Produced by Copyright
Graphic conception : Ute-Charlotte Hettler
Layout : Odile Delaporte
Cover : Yannick Le Bourg
Editorial Collaboration : Isabelle Raimond